MW01248777

He Can't Make You Happy

Discover The Reasons Why

SKIP BAILEY

To. Trikita
Be Happy
Skip B.

Copyright © 2017 by Skip Bailey

ISBN: 978-1-5323-3480-1

All Rights Reserved. No part of this book may be reproduced or
transmitted in any form or by any means, electronic or mechanical,
including photocopying, recording, or by any information storage and
retrieval system without written permission from the author, except for
the inclusion of brief quotations in a review.

Printed in the United States of America.

TABLE OF CONTENTS

DEDICATION

This book is dedicated to women from all walks of life and from all nationalities, ethnic groups, and backgrounds. You are very special women, and you deserve all of the information available to you to assist you in becoming the women you were created to be. This book is also dedicated to the women in my family, because I see the strength in you. If this book can help you to become stronger women, then this is my gift to you. This book is especially dedicated to my fiancée, Yvette; my mother, Tina Bailey; and to my daughter, Toya. Thank you for always supporting me in my projects, books, and events. Your support means so much to me; I am ever so grateful and I appreciate you.

INTRODUCTION

This book was written to help women discover their inner strength and to assist you in finding your own happiness and joy. Some women are constantly struggling with what's going on in their relationships. This also applies to marriage. Many things in life may not exactly go as planned. Have you often wondered why he can't make you happy? Does he even want you to be happy or to be happy with you? Do you sometimes find yourself going out of your way to make him happy, and that doesn't make him happy, either? Have you found yourself blaming him for your not being happy or find yourself saying, "He just don't understand what I'm going through"? In *He Can't Make You Happy*, you will discover a lot of answers for these questions.

You will discover some things about yourself that will help you understand why he can't make you happy. You will get to know and understand that you've had the answers all along, but you didn't know where to look. Look no further, because in this book you will find answers to those questions. Use this book to help you find your happiness, your joy, your peace of mind, and a happy heart. Read this book several times, because you may not absorb all the information the first or second time reading it.

By all means, please share the information in this book by purchasing a copy(s) for a friend or a loved one. By doing so, you will be helping someone who may be experiencing similar situations. Do someone a huge favor and pass it on.

SESSION 1

WHAT STORY ARE YOU TELLING?

WHAT STORIES ARE YOU TELLING yourself and other people? Is the story that you're telling the real truth about what's going on in your life? It may be your perception and your reality, but is it the truth? We often change the script of our lives and situation so that we begin to believe that, no matter what the truth and facts are, we will see what we want to see. For example, you may be in a relationship with someone who has not been faithful in past relationships. You get involved with him, and someone tells you that they've seen him sitting in a restaurant talking with another lady. You immediately confront him, and he tells you that the lady is a relative. Two weeks later, you happen to see him talking to the same woman, and the woman is really beautiful. Immediately, you begin to tell yourself made-up stories about what is going on. You confront him. The truth is that the woman he was having lunch with is actually a relative, and she has been helping him with a project. The stories that you have been telling yourself caused you to be suspicious, upset, and maybe even angry. He may ask you why you didn't confront him when it was first brought to your attention instead of waiting until later.

Maybe a past relationship of your own is causing you to distrust the person that you are involved with now. The stories and beliefs from your past are causing you to bring negative baggage into your current relationships; this is baggage that you may not be aware of. I say *relationships* because this baggage can and will affect all of your relationships, including romantic relationships, friendships, business relationships, and social relationships. You might ask, what do friendships, business, and social relationships have to do with the fact that he can't make me happy? I am glad that you asked that question. Keep reading, and you will find the answers in the upcoming classes.

So, my question to you is, what story or stories are you telling yourself? What stories have you told yourself in the past? I'm not just talking about romance stories; I'm talking about stories of your life. I'm talking about stories that do not involve "him"; these stories are about you.

NOTES

_____

_____

_____

_____

_____

_____

_____

_____

_____

_____

_____

_____

_____

SESSION 2

WHO IS THE WOMAN IN THE MIRROR?

YOU SEE YOURSELF IN THE mirror every day, and at times you may ask yourself "Who am I?" It may be early in the book, but it's time to be honest with yourself. You may put on a front for other people and tell them that you know who you are, but do you really know who you are? I'm not talking about your exterior; I'm talking about your inner self. I'm talking about your deep-down honest knowledge of who you are. Some people may not have discovered who the person is that they see in the mirror each morning. Many individuals go through their entire lives not knowing who they really are and not knowing why they do most of the things that they do. I've heard people say that they have done something out of character, and when asked why they did the action, the answer was "I don't know." I've heard comments such as "He (or she)

5

made me angry or frustrated and caused me to do what I did."
No one can make you do anything without your allowing it.

So, the question is "Who is the woman in the mirror?" If
answering that question seems to be a challenge for you, I am
here to tell you that it may not be totally your fault for not being
able to completely answer it. You may attempt to answer the
question to the best of your knowledge, but there may be things
about you—or things in your life—that cause the answer to
be hidden. Sometimes, people are programmed or raised to
become the people that their parents want them to be, and
they totally dismiss thoughts of who they want to be or the type
of individual that they desire to become. If this information is
causing you to really think about what is being said and causes
you to say "hmmm," then keep reading, and you will discover
things that you weren't aware of or didn't know.

NOTES

_____

_____

_____

_____

_____

_____

_____

_____

_____

_____

_____

_____

_____

SESSION 3

WHERE DID "IT" COME FROM?

WHERE DID IT ALL COME from, and when did it start—"It" meaning where did all of the thinking and reasoning come from? Are you aware that many times we are reacting from the people, places, and things that we encounter each day? People, places, and things that we are connected to daily play a major part in our lives, and we are not aware of it.

Let's start with people. The people that you are in contact with on a regular basis are becoming a part of you, and you are also becoming a part of them. For instance, you begin to pick up the actions and habits of the friends and associates with which you spend a considerable amount of time. If you and your best friend are together frequently, you will start acting like each other, talking like each other, and sometimes even looking like each other. You may not notice this about yourself, but I'm sure that you've noticed it in other people. You often notice children acting like their parents or spouses acting like each other, but if no one has ever brought it to your attention, you may have never noticed it about yourself.

Do you act similar to someone? It may be your mother, father, friend, someone you're in a relationship with, or your spouse.

Some of the places that you frequently go may have an effect on the way you think and do things. If you are constantly in unhealthy environments, you will be affected by that environment. For instance, if you are going to places where negative issues are often displayed, after a while those negative issues will begin to affect you.

Things will have an effect on you, too. This is something that you may not want to hear, but constantly watching negative talk shows and negative reality shows will definitely have an effect on you. If you watch shows where there is arguing, cheating, or fighting, you will be affected. This is like putting poison into your system. You are poisoning your brain with negative situations, which is altering your thinking. Just like individuals who put drugs into their bodies, you are doing the same thing. There may not be any outer physical evidence, but you can be sure that there are inner issues. Having those inner issues can and will have an effect on your happiness.

NOTES

_____

_____

_____

_____

_____

_____

_____

_____

_____

_____

_____

_____

_____

_____

SESSION 4

WHAT IS THE REAL TRUTH?

HAT'S THE REAL TRUTH ABOUT you, and what's the truth about what is going on in your life? At this moment, I'm assuming that you are reading this book by yourself and not reading it out loud or to someone else. Being that you are reading it alone, what's the real truth about you?

You don't have to try to impress anyone or put on a front for anyone; it's just you and these pages. Right now, you can think of me as your Personal Life Coach, and you can begin to release the truth. Sometimes, we tell ourselves lies about what's really going on with our lives and situations; then, we begin to believe those lies. The lies that we tell ourselves become so normal that we begin telling other people the same stories just to validate ourselves.

If you keep telling yourself the same stories, you will keep getting the same results. It's time for you to get totally real with yourself. You can now stop pretending that everything in your life is perfect when you know there are many areas in your life that need fixing. I say "fixing" because there are areas in many of our lives that are broken, and it is time to stop overlooking and covering up what really needs immediate attention.

You may have heard the saying "We need to find our roots." I'm here to tell you that you need to find the roots in your life. You need to go back as far as you can remember and find your roots, and I'm not talking about your family history roots. I'm referring to your own personal roots. If you discover your personal roots, I am sure that you will begin to find your real truth—the truth about why things in your life have been moving in the direction that they have so far; the truth about how and why you've made some of your past decisions; the truth in possibly understanding why you've chosen some of your relationships. If you don't say it to anyone else, it's time to discover and tell yourself the truth.

NOTES

_____

_____

_____

_____

_____

_____

_____

_____

_____

_____

_____

_____

_____

_____

SESSION 5

IT'S YOU AND ONLY YOU

I T'S YOU AND ONLY YOU who can tell your story. You may think that others have your story down pack and reflect on your life the way you may have displayed it, but again, it's you and only you. Have you ever said to yourself that people just don't understand you? I've often heard individuals make that statement. One of the reasons that you and other individuals may think and feel that way is because sometimes you may not totally understand yourself. Now don't get offended: I'm only trying to help. By the way, you are not the only one. Many people have experienced the same things that you have experienced or may be experiencing about yourself. Most individuals are constantly in the presence of others and are distracted by things other than their own lives, so they never get to know what's really going on with themselves. You may be so distracted by your cell phone, social media, work, television, family, or life that you may forget what has taken place in your life or what is happening in and with your life.

It is time to pump your brakes and start reflecting on your past and present life.

Your past is not your present, but your past may have led you to your current present. Your past experiences may have caused or may be causing your current life situation(s) to be what it is. There may have been situations in your past that are still causing you to hold onto unpleasant feelings and unpleasant thoughts. Those feelings and thoughts can sometimes cause pain in your life and in your relationships. Your past is your past; now, it's time to leave your past where it belongs (in the past). It's you and only you who can let it go and move forward. It's you who can forgive your past, if that's what you must do. It is you who can forgive yourself, if that's what you need to do. This may require you to seek professional coaching to help you along the way, but you can and you must do it. I say this may require seeking professional life coaching because, like so many individuals, you may have a friend, a cousin, or maybe a hairstylist or bartender, but it's not working, is it?

By the time you finish reading *He Can't Make You Happy*, you will notice a huge change in the way you think of and see yourself.

NOTES

_____

_____

_____

_____

_____

_____

_____

_____

_____

_____

_____

_____

_____

SESSION 6

GET OFF YOUR PITY POT

B Y NOW, YOU MAY HAVE noticed that this book is not really about him making you happy, and you may be right. As you continue to read, though, you will discover that it has never been about him or anyone else making you happy.

This is where it gets real about you, your life, and your happiness. So, don't get upset with what you are reading because this has been happening for a long time. I've not so long ago discovered what was causing some of my life's issues and challenges. Most of what you are experiencing is likely not your fault; you probably didn't cause it. However, once you discover the causes and the root, it's your responsibility to change and fix them. If you have had negative thoughts and self-doubt, it's time to discontinue that thinking. It's time to get off your pity pot. It's time to start finding your true answers and giving yourself what you and only you can give yourself. No one was created to make you happy, and no one can make you happy—not your boyfriend, not your spouse, not even your parents or siblings.

No one but you was created to fulfill your happiness. Others may add to your happiness, but it is up to you to fill your happiness cup. I keep referring to your past: Maybe your childhood or your teenage years reflect your current relationships and situations. Maybe you sometimes feel that you missed out on something in your life as you were growing up. Whatever it may be, as long as you keep searching for answers to find your truth, you will be amazed at what you'll discover. Here's a word of advice: Do not go on a search for negative things, but just search for the unanswered truth. A professional life coach can help you tap into the answers that you seek.

From now on, do not get on the pity pot, and don't start any more pity parties, because pity parties don't provide any positive and sustainable solutions and answers. Seek some help and be happy.

NOTES

SESSION 7

HE CAN'T GIVE YOU WHAT HE DOESN'T HAVE

URING MY CONVERSATIONS WITH WOMEN, they have stated on many occasions that "he doesn't really give me what I want and need." One of the reasons that he can't give you what you want is because he doesn't have "it" to give. Whether you know it or not—and maybe he doesn't know it, either—he has issues, too. Maybe his male ego or his pride is preventing him from viewing his deep-down issues. He may have some of the same issues as you. Have there been times when you attempted to get your partner to open up and express himself, and he would reply "I'm good" or "nothing's wrong with me"? In most cases, he wasn't taught that opening up and expressing himself is a good thing. Many guys are taught that opening up is a sign of weakness, and that it's best to keep it to themselves. There may have been things that happened in their lives or things and situations that they wished had happened. There may be things that they wish had not happened, such as being bullied, getting into trouble, not doing well in school, or experimenting with drugs.

He could have witnessed his parents arguing and fighting or he may have experienced a lot of family issues. He may have had pressure put on him to do as well as his siblings, friends, or other individuals. He may have forgotten some things because he buried the issues deep within himself, just to ease the pain. I use the word *pain* because some men have buried pain, and they sometimes act out of anger and are not aware of the real cause.

Perhaps he wanted his father to spend more time with him. Many men are carrying around hurt and pain because they haven't bonded with their fathers. Unfortunately, many fathers are not involved in their sons' lives due to separation from the family for various reasons. Some men have seen their fathers move on to other relationships, become incarcerated, die, or spend more time with their jobs and careers than facing their responsibilities.

This can and does have a major impact on their sons. Sometimes, the sons carry the hurt and pain into other relationships.

Some of this hurt and pain can be due to "mother" issues. For the most part, though, these issues could have been addressed and maybe handled by a father's participation.

So, now that you are in a relationship with a guy who has some issues, you may have noticed him becoming upset or frustrated. This could be an effect from his past.

Has there been an incident when your partner exploded with anger toward you? The two of you may have had a small disagreement, and out of nowhere he took it to another level; that may have been some of those deep issues surfacing. He's probably not aware of where that explosion came from at the moment; all he knows is that he is angry.

You need to understand that he has issues, too. To be straightforward and totally honest with you, his issues are more of a challenge to accept and to deal with than yours.

I say that because of some facts: You can talk to your cousin, your friend, or even your hairstylist. You may not always take their advice, but you will seek out other people. For the most part, your partner won't. He will keep it bottled up inside for a long time, and that can lead to even more pain.

Men have feelings, too, but they have not learned how to express their feelings and emotions in the proper way. Instead of men seeking advice from their cousins, friends, or barbers, they will sometimes turn to alcohol, drugs, or another female. If his deeply embedded issues are surfacing on a regular basis, chances are that he may have been avoiding those issues for quite some time. I am not saying that this is always the case, but it's not far from it.

Most men will not consult a professional life coach, just as a lot women won't, either. But you will be doing yourself a favor in seeking a professional life coach to help with your self-healing process.

You may say that I used the word *self-healing*, so why do I need a life coach? Being straightforward again: The purpose of a life coach is to help guide and assist you, because if you could have done it on your own, you would have done it already.

You may say that I am telling it all and not holding anything back. In order for me to help you, it is my duty and obligation to do that.

I want you to understand that this class is not a snitching or bashing class; it's just helping you to understand and relate to men a little better. Whether it's your partner, your spouse, your brother, or even your father, there are similarities in almost all men.

I must also say this: Even if you've noticed questionable behavior from your brother or father, you might want to refer to this class again. The nerve of me: First, I refer to issues concerning your partner or spouse, and now I'm including your father or brother. What in the world is wrong with Skip? There is nothing wrong with me, but there are certainly a lot of things right with me now, being that I've discovered things mentioned in this class.

I mentioned earlier that men are not taught to express their feelings and emotions because that's not a sign of being tough. Well, not expressing themselves as they should has caused a lot of men to make unwise decisions and experience unpleasant situations. If the information in this class had been revealed to young men, then maybe those situations would not have happened.

I hope that you are absorbing the information that you are reading in this class. Not only can you began to understand some issues your partner, spouse, brother, or father may have gone through or may be going through, but this may also help you understand and relate to your son, if you have a son. Even if you don't have a son but you know of someone who has a son(s), please share this information with them. That's part of our purpose, which is to share, help, and pass it on.

Notes

_____

_____

_____

_____

_____

_____

_____

_____

_____

_____

_____

_____

_____

SESSION 8

HE IS NOT YOUR DADDY

AS MENTIONED EARLIER, IT IS time to refocus on what's going on with you. This class is titled "He Is Not Your Daddy" because you may want and expect your partner to do certain things that you've always imagined having and experiencing. Ok, it's straight-talk time again, and this talk has two sides. First, if you were raised in a household with your father being in your life from birth through childhood and into adulthood, that's great for you. If your father oftentimes spoiled you, as most fathers do when it comes to their precious daughters, then you should consider yourself fortunate. Your father most likely attended your special events, such as your dance recitals, your sports games, and maybe even walked you down the aisle on your wedding day. But if your situation was the total opposite, some of the issues that you may be experiencing might lie there because there are so many women who don't know the feeling or what it's like to have the continuous love of a father. That's where some of the problems may occur when it comes to your relationships. Some women may expect the same type of love and attention from her partner or spouse that she received from her loving father. On the other hand, some women may expect the type of love and attention that they did not receive from their father.

This is a sensitive subject, so I'm going to be honest but not as straight-in-your-face. As stated in the last class ("He Can't Give You What He Doesn't Have"), he can't give you what your father did not give you, either. He can only give you his love and attention, not your father's love. You may just be discovering what you have been missing in your life, so don't put pressure on your partner concerning an issue of which he's unaware. If this is your issue, one of the best things that you can do is to explain to him what has been bothering you and causing you grief. The fact that you've been talking about it will begin to release some unpleasant feelings and thoughts that you've been holding onto.

NOTES

_____

_____

_____

_____

_____

_____

_____

_____

_____

_____

_____

_____

_____

SESSION 9

PUSHING HIM AWAY

I F YOU FIND YOURSELF SEEKING fatherly love and affection from your partner, he may begin to feel pressured. Remember what we spoke of earlier: He can't give you what he doesn't have, and he definitely doesn't have the same love and affection that you've been seeking from your father. Sometimes, people compare their relationships to the relationships of others, and they expect their partners to do the same things that they see in other relationships. That's another way he may feel pressured, and that will certainly not bring him closer to you. Here's my final example because I don't want to seem as though I am pointing the finger only at you. We all have faults, but if you are constantly pointing out his faults and not looking at your own, you may be pushing him away without even knowing it. You may have just as many or maybe even more faults yourself, but you are always focusing on his; that's not good for your relationship. We are going to end this class because I believe that you are beginning to learn and understand that there is so much growth ahead of you. As long as you read and absorb the information in this book, you will continue to grow and become the woman that you were created to be.

NOTES

_____

_____

_____

_____

_____

_____

_____

_____

_____

_____

_____

_____

_____

_____

SESSION 10

YOU CAN'T GIVE WHAT YOU DON'T HAVE

IN YOUR RELATIONSHIP, YOUR PARTNER may be seeking some of the same things that you are seeking. He may be seeking the love and affection that he didn't get from his parents. Maybe he wasn't raised by his mother but was raised by another family member, such as a grandmother, or maybe his father didn't spend much time with him. This man might have missed out on some motherly love, which he has been yearning for all of his life. Maybe his mother has never been in his life or maybe his mother had her own issues and didn't do what is expected of a mother. Situations such as this can have a major impact on the emotions and mindset of a young child or teenager. The same goes for you. If you are dealing with some of the issues that were mentioned in the previous classes, not only can't you give him what you don't have, but you can't begin to give yourself what you haven't totally acknowledged and accepted.

My hope for you is that you apply all the information on these pages and begin to become the outstanding person that you really want to be. You can only give him what you have now, but after completing these classes, you can and will begin to give more of what and who you really are. It's not just wishing and wanting things to change in your life and in your relationships; you must change. I'm not saying that you must change for him. You must change for yourself. Whether you're in a romantic relationship or in any other relationship, you must change you first.

Notes

_____

_____

_____

_____

_____

_____

_____

_____

_____

_____

_____

_____

SESSION 11

YOU GET WHAT YOU TOLERATE

DO YOU OFTEN FIND YOURSELF getting the same results in certain situations? Do you tolerate things or actions that you totally disagree with or know that you shouldn't accept? Do you accept things that people say or do, knowing that you may have been offended, but your reason for not responding is that you don't want to offend anyone, yourself? Without responding in a negative manner, you must begin to protect yourself and your feelings. No longer should you tolerate anything that may cause you to feel inferior. No longer should you tolerate spending your time with people who aren't growing or going in the same direction as you. No longer should you do the things that aren't helping you grow and move toward your greatness. As a matter of fact, you shouldn't tolerate more excuses or negative thinking from yourself, either—no more lying to yourself, no more cheating yourself, and no more limiting yourself. If you agree to not lie, cheat, or limit yourself, then by all means don't tolerate those things from anyone else, either. You are phenomenal and you are a child of the Most High.

You are a winner, you are a champion, you are an achiever, and you can do anything that you set your mind and heart to, but never tolerate less from yourself. Once you begin to not tolerate those limiting things, other people will notice that you have your "no tolerance" guard up. It's not that you have to go around as if you have a guard up at all times. It's just that, in most cases, people know who and who not to mess with. This can be anywhere—at work, at school, at home, and even in a relationship; when and when not to test your tolerance level will be obvious to the other person. At no time should you give someone permission to test your tolerance level.

NOTES

_____

_____

_____

_____

_____

_____

_____

_____

_____

_____

_____

_____

_____

Notes

SESSION 12

SHOPPING WON'T MAKE YOU HAPPY

EOPLE OFTEN DO THINGS THAT they think will help fix the situations that they are experiencing. Some would say shopping is a quick fix for the moment and that it's not long term. I'm here to tell you that shopping is just a momentary distraction that will eventually give you only a temporary sense of satisfaction. I want you to notice that I said "temporary sense of satisfaction," not satisfaction, because it will not satisfy what you've been yearning for. I'm not trying to "burst you bubble," as the saying goes. I'm just giving you information as it should be given—without sugar coating. If I sugar-coat the information in this book, then I will be wasting your time and my time. I hope that you can, and will, appreciate the fact that I am not holding back punches and that I have your best interest at hand. My wish for you is that, when you finish reading *He Can't Make You*

Happy, you will have a totally different perspective and a new outlook on how and why certain things are the way they are.

Don't mislead yourself into thinking, and maybe even believing, that shopping will make things better, because it doesn't and it won't. Maybe you've heard some women say, "I'm going shopping. It will make me feel better." If that is true, why is it that when reality sets in, the feeling is sometimes worse? Shopping is just what it is—to purchase an item that you may want or that you've wanted—and that's all that shopping is. Some people shop so much and so often that stuff begins to accumulate in their homes. At times, they may have asked themselves "Why did I buy this; I didn't need it." You probably didn't need the item(s), but at the moment you weren't thinking of whether you needed it or not; you were just looking for a temporary fix. So, the next time you find yourself in a situation where you feel that you need to shop in order to feel better, stop and ask yourself "Will this fix my situation?" I can almost guarantee that the answer will be "no."

By now you should be starting to understand that no matter what happens, or what situations you encounter, it's you and only you who can make things better in your life. Shopping can't fix or change things; drinking won't do it; getting involved in another relationship can't do it; and even changing locations won't do it. It is you who truly has the answer(s) to your situation(s). All you may need is a little professional coaching, and you'll be surprised at how quickly your situation will change. We put bandages on wounds, cuts, and bruises to protect the affected area while it is healing. The bandage does not heal the affected area; the wound heals itself. Just as shopping may be your bandage, it may also be your protection for the moment, but you must heal yourself—something that shopping can't and never will be able to do.

NOTES

_____

_____

_____

_____

_____

_____

_____

_____

_____

_____

_____

_____

_____

SESSION 13

EMPTY YOUR JAR

W

E NOW COME TO THE part where it's time to empty your jar, meaning that it's time to get rid of all things that have caused you to feel the way you've felt in the past. It's almost like detoxing and cleansing yourself of all of the negative stuff that you've stored in your physical and spiritual life. If you've ever drunk detox tea, then you should have an idea of what I'm talking about. Oftentimes, people consume so many unhealthy foods and beverages that, after a while, those things begin to have a negative effect on their bodies. Once you begin to detox your body with detox tea, though, you'll begin to rid your body of bad stuff that has been in your system for a long time.

By emptying your jar, you will begin to rid yourself of the negative people, places, and things from your life. Whether you've been carrying this negativity around with you for 1 year, 10 years, 20 years, or even longer, by emptying your jar you will have space for healthfulness to enter. We will talk more about the good stuff in Session 15.

Another example would be looking into a glass jar of dirty water that has not been changed for years. The glass jar may have had all types of dirty stuff in it, and it may not ever have been changed or cleaned. As more dirt falls into the jar on top of existing dirt, the jar keeps getting worse. By not emptying your jar, you are pretty much doing the same thing; you are letting all of your past negative feelings, thoughts, and emotions pile on top of your current negative feelings, thoughts, and emotions. You or someone that you know may be experiencing unpleasant emotions and situations at the moment, and they may be wondering why it seems so difficult. It could be that old dirt is piling on top of your current dirt, and it's making the situation seem even more difficult.

Write down all the negative feelings that you are experiencing, whether they're from your childhood, your early adulthood, or your current situation. You must put it all down on paper, no matter what it was or is, because this is the beginning of letting go and beginning the healing process.

This is where you must be totally honest with yourself, even if you've never allowed yourself to be totally honest in the past. I've said "honest" a couple of times because, during this process, you don't have to be concerned with the thoughts of someone else.

At this very moment, it's you and only you. You can and should write down what you really feel and what you honestly think about yourself. After you have completed your writing, take some time to read and reflect on what you have written. Take as long as you need, because after you finish reading, it will be time to move to the next session.

In the next session, you will write down everything that you intend to let go. This will be your "let it go" list. This is where you begin to empty your jar by letting go of all the things that have caused you to feel the way you have in the past. If it's certain people, let them go; if it's places, let them go; and if it's things, by all means let them go. Don't hold onto anything that has caused you feel any less than you've always wanted to feel, and I do believe that you've been wanting good, happy, and pleasant feelings for a long time. You should read your let-it-go list a few times so that you can begin to release your unwanted past experiences, feelings, and thoughts.

After you've read your let-it-go list, BURN IT, RELEASE IT, EMPTY YOUR JAR, AND LET IT GO.

Notes

_____

_____

_____

_____

_____

_____

_____

_____

_____

_____

_____

_____

_____

_____

SESSION 14

HIT YOUR RESET BUTTON

NOW THAT YOU'VE EXPERIENCED THE previous classes, it's time to hit your reset button. I will use the analogy of a desktop or laptop computer. At times, we may have issues with our computer and may not know what's going on with it. We may have tried several different approaches, but after trying these, we find that all we had to do was hit the reset or refresh button. After emptying your jar—meaning starting to get rid of all the negative thoughts and issues that you've been carrying around—it's time for a restart. You can start focusing on the positive things and the new things that you want in your life. You start to go places that you've wanted to go in the past, but your thinking would not lead you in that direction. Remember, if you constantly think it and believe it, you become it, no matter what it is.

This may be challenging. Hitting your reset button may require you to spend less time with some people and more time with others. I'm talking about some individuals who may appear to be friends and even some family members.

You may wonder if you're spending less time with some of these people, then who are you going hang with? If those individuals are not contributing to your growth, it's time to climb higher and surround yourself with people who will contribute to your growth. Billions of people are in the world; I'm quite sure that you can find someone somewhere. As the saying goes, "Seek and ye shall find."

Let's hit the reset button, get this new thing started, and begin to move forward. Just as you may have to sometimes hit the reset or refresh button on your laptop, you may also have to hit your own reset button a few times. As long you keep trying and never give up, something good is going to happen for you.

NOTES

_____

_____

_____

_____

_____

_____

_____

_____

_____

_____

_____

SESSION 15

REFILL YOUR JAR

NOW IT'S TIME TO REFILL your jar (your life) with all of the wonderful things that you deserve to have. It's time to fill yourself and your life with all of the love and inner beauty that you've been seeking. The love that I am speaking of is the inner love that no one else can give you. The only person who can give you that kind of love is you, and your higher power. The love that I'm talking about is the love that your husband/companion can't give you; your mother or father can't give it to you; and not even your children can give it to you. It's self-love that I'm speaking of, not conceit. It's filling yourself with all of the love and joy that you've always wanted to experience.

Now that you are beginning to know that it's possible, you can prepare yourself for a new and wonderful journey. You will be amazed with the unlimited amount of self-love, joy, and inner satisfaction that you begin to feel.

One thing that will help you along your new journey is to take a walk through a park filled with trees and flowers. Allowing yourself to experience the beauty of nature will help you to begin your journey toward self-love and joy. Nature has a way of doing things that we sometimes can't explain. Do yourself a favor and take a nature walk.

NOTES

_____

_____

_____

_____

_____

_____

_____

_____

_____

_____

_____

_____

_____

_____

SESSION 16

REJECT THE BS

EJECTING BS IS ONE AREA that must be monitored at all times. BS is something that you may have been involved with in the past. It can happen anywhere and at any given time. If you have experienced BS on a regular basis in the past, be aware that people, places, and things may still be connected to BS. Sometimes, you may have to pass through BS on your journey to bettering yourself, but just remember to keep moving; do not get caught or stuck in BS. If at any time one of those individuals whom you're spending less time with is trying to get you to participate in BS, reject that BS. If you were involved in a relationship in the past, and the relationship led to BS, most likely the same BS has a chance of recurring.

This is serious stuff because being involved with BS did not get you to a good place in the past, and BS will not get you anywhere in the future. Many people are in BS, and many of them aren't even aware of it because they've become accustomed to BS. For many people, the BS has become normal and part of their everyday lives.

So for you, my friend, let's keep your BS detector on alert at all times. I am not saying to live your life on the edge, but be conscious of whom and what you'll allow into your life.

By the way, I don't know what you were thinking, but BS means Bad Situations.

NOTES

_____

_____

_____

_____

_____

_____

_____

_____

_____

_____

_____

_____

_____

SESSION 17

DON'T SETTLE FOR LESS FROM YOURSELF

YOU'VE PROBABLY SETTLED FOR LESS from other people or maybe from certain situations but, by all means, don't settle for less from yourself. Settling and accepting less from yourself is only giving yourself permission to continue the same situations that you've already experienced.

Let's take a look at a few examples. You may have gone to a restaurant and the food or service was not satisfactory, but you didn't mention it to the manager; you just accepted things as they were. That was a situation of you settling for less, in which you could have received better service. Maybe you purchased an item from a store, and when you got home, the item wasn't what you expected. Instead of driving back to the store, you may have settled for the item because it wasn't worth the drive back to the store. This is another example of settling for less.

By now, you should have begun to realize your worth, and you should not settle for less. You should know what you deserve, what you really want, and what you do not want. In the last class, we talked about rejecting BS. From now on, reject your own BS, and this time I'm not talking about bad situations; you know what I'm talking about.

I really don't mean to offend by being so straightforward, but some of us, even me at times, need straightforward talk. Sometimes, being straightforward is what will get through to us. At times we can be so blind to the things we are involved in that it takes straight talk to get us to realize our own truth. So, we settle for less and lie to ourselves, even though in our true heart of hearts we know the truth, and we know we can and should do better.

Let's continue to move forward, as we know that we can, and live our lives to the fullest. If you need help and coaching, by all means, ask for it.

Notes

_____

_____

_____

_____

_____

_____

_____

_____

_____

_____

_____

_____

SESSION 18

LOVE AND APPRECIATE YOURSELF

M Y QUESTION TO YOU IS: Do you love yourself? I mean, do you really love yourself and do you appreciate yourself? We oftentimes find ourselves telling other people that we love and appreciate them, but how often do we feel love and appreciation for ourselves? I know that it's not normal for individuals to tell themselves that they love themselves, but believe me, it is quite okay to do so. I am not talking about being self-centered or being conceited; I'm talking about your having true love for you. Many top professional life coaches and empowerment specialists say that they recommend individuals to look at themselves in a mirror and say to themselves, "I love you." This is such a powerful experience that it may feel a little uncomfortable the first time you do it. But as you begin to do this exercise on a regular basis, and as you look into your eyes, saying those three words to yourself, you will begin feel a real inner connection.

Let's pause for a few minutes, and if you are near a mirror, give it a try. Go ahead and do it: You have nothing to lose, and you will only gain. Look yourself in the eye, not looking at your hair or even your makeup—just your eyes. This will take focus and concentration. Now say, "I love you." It feels a little different, doesn't it? If you've done the exercise, congratulations. However, if you have not done so, give it a try when you are ready.

One of the greatest feelings that can be experienced is the feeling of self-love and self-appreciation. By my writing these few words, I am experiencing my own self-love and self-appreciation. We oftentimes give so much of ourselves to others that we neglect ourselves. Continue to show and give love and appreciation to others, but also remember to love and appreciate yourself.

NOTES

SESSION 19

DARE TO DREAM

THIS IS WHERE YOU BEGIN to step out and step up in your life. You should be at the point where you start to dream. Dreaming is visualizing the type of life that you want to live. Many people have stopped dreaming about the life/lifestyle that they truly want and have always wanted for themselves. While going through life, we often get dreams smashed by life's challenges and situations. Oftentimes, we put our dreams and aspirations on hold because of our responsibilities, such as family, securing employment, or maybe being a caregiver for a loved one. Those things are important, because if you have responsibilities, then you are supposed to take care of those responsibilities. I often speak with people who have done the things that they were supposed to do, but their dreams seem to no longer exist. I know individuals whose children are grown and have their own lives, but the majority of individuals will not live their dreams.

It is said that one of the richest places on earth is the graveyard; that statement was made because so many people did not attempt to live their dreams. The majority of people have their dreams buried in their grave with them. Don't arrive at the end of your physical life and not attempt to live your dreams.

Let's have a quick reality check: As long as your dreams are realistic, then I say go for it. Reality check: If your dream was to be a professional basketball player and you are in your 30s, 40s, or 50s, I hope that you are getting my point. But don't be discouraged; we were blessed with many talents and gifts. You may be in your 30s, 40s, or 50s and you've always dreamed of being a professional chef. With that type of dream, there are unlimited resources and opportunities. Besides, most of the best cooks and professional chefs are of the ages mentioned.

In some cases, you may have talents and gifts that you are not aware of. You may have untapped talents and gifts that are just waiting to be bought to life by you, and only you. For instance, I'd never even thought of writing a book, but this is my second book. My first book, *You Are Outstanding and Unstoppable*, was published a little over 2½ years ago. I was sitting at work one summer night, and God give me a thought and a title of a book. After *You Are Outstanding and Unstoppable* was published, I would often say that I had no desire to write another book. But God knows best, because here is book number two, and this is how it came to be.

I was on the telephone with my brother in July 2016. I was saying to him that I did not want or need anything for my birthday, which is what I also told my fiancée and my mother. After reaffirming that I really did not want or need anything for my birthday, here it came—another book title, *He Can't Make You Happy*.

76

This is what I believe was my gift from God. This book is my gift, and I am directed to share it with individuals who are seeking answers to unresolved questions. One of my blessings is to gift you and many other people with the gifts that I'm receiving. Even though the title of this book is *He Can't Make You Happy*, by no means is this book a male-bashing or a tell-all book. It is about telling you what you should and need to know regarding some of the issues that you may have. This book is life coaching in a book format.

It's time to take another pause to reflect on some of your dreams, desires, and aspirations. Have there been times when you were planning to do something and said, "I'll put it down here and get to it later"? Is that same thing that you put to the side a year ago, still sitting there waiting to be moved or taken care of? Don't be ashamed to admit it: It's ok; you're not the only one. I've done it, too. By daring to dream again, this process is one of the things that will help you with your own happiness. So, take a break from reading for a few minutes and write some of your dreams, desires, and aspirations on the note sheet.

Notes

_____

_____

_____

_____

_____

_____

_____

_____

_____

_____

_____

_____

_____

SESSION 20

LIVE YOUR DREAMS

NOW IT'S TIME TO LIVE your dreams and not look back. Looking back too often distracts you from where you are headed. As you drive your car, you are supposed to focus on what's going on in your front windshield and not as much focus on the rear windshield. That's why the front windshield is larger than the rear windshield, so that you can focus on where you are going and not focus on where you have been.

Reflect on the things that you've written on your note sheets; now it's time to put those things into action. It's not enough to just dream and write your thoughts on paper; you *must* take action. If I hadn't written this entire book and forwarded it to the publishing company, you would not be holding it in your hand.

Whatever your dreams, desires, and aspirations are, take action and make it happen. If your dreams are to become a chef, do your research. If you cannot afford the classes yet, go to YouTube to view techniques, styles, and information pertaining to your desired choice. When you go to restaurants, observe the way the foods are displayed on your plate. I am a musician and that's what I do quite often. Before I acquired the instrument that I perform with, I did a lot of research on YouTube. When I would go to concerts, even if I had great seats, I would take my binoculars to get a close look at every instrument and name brand that was played. So, whatever dreams, desires, and aspirations you have, don't cheat yourself any longer. Don't hold back, go for it, and go get it.

NOTES

_____

_____

_____

_____

_____

_____

_____

_____

_____

_____

_____

_____

_____

Notes

SESSION 21

FIND YOUR HAPPINESS/
LIVE YOUR HAPPINESS

INDING YOUR HAPPINESS IS EASIER than you may believe it to be. By now, you know that no one but you can make you happy, and no one can find your happiness but you. Other people can assist you in different areas of your life, but finding your happiness is your job and your responsibility. You are responsible for uncovering the joy that you have inside of you. Your happiness and joy are major components in achieving inner peace.

There is a story that is told: When God created man and women, he was searching for a place to put happiness and joy. There were a couple of suggestions from a few angels. One angel suggested that God put happiness on the tallest mountain in the world, but God said that sooner or later it would be found. Another angel suggested putting happiness at the bottom of the deepest ocean, but God said that it would also be found. Then God said, "I'll put happiness and joy inside man and woman. They will look every other place, other than looking inside themselves for happiness and joy." (Author Unknown)

I hope that you caught the hint regarding where to find your happiness and joy. So, don't look in the mall on the shoe rack or on the handbag stand. It's not on your favorite television show or in that glass of wine. Your happiness lies inside of you and nowhere else. Now find your happiness and joy and begin to be happy and joyful; it is such an awesome feeling. Smile and be happy !

NOTES

_____

_____

_____

_____

_____

_____

_____

_____

_____

_____

_____

_____

SESSION 22

BELIEVE IN YOURSELF

D<small>ID YOU KNOW THAT THERE</small> are individuals who believe in other people and in other things more than they believe in themselves? There are people who believe more in their boss than they believe in themselves. They may even believe more in the characters on their favorite television show. Some individuals think that their self-belief system does not exist. So, I am asking you, what is your belief level in yourself and in your life? Have you lost belief in yourself, and you feel that your self-belief is gone forever? What do you believe about yourself at this very moment, and at this moment, how do you feel about yourself? I am guessing that at this point you're starting that self-belief system back on the upward trail. I am even guessing that, at least, there is some hope and desire to continue to gain or regain your self-belief; otherwise, you wouldn't be still reading this book. I'm also guessing that you are curious about how things will be different for you and your life. There maybe even a slight smile on your face. I can almost say for certain that you are seeking self-belief, and you want more self-belief in your life. Just keep working on yourself and read this book again because you will pick up things that you may have missed in your first reading. Say to yourself a few times before you go to sleep: I BELIEVE IN MYSELF. This will begin to do more than you can imagine. So, DO IT!

NOTES

_____

_____

_____

_____

_____

_____

_____

_____

_____

_____

_____

_____

_____

SESSION 23

LET GO AND LET GOD

THIS WILL BE SHORT AND straight to the point. Let go and let God. Who and whatever your higher power may be, let your higher power take control. We often try to do certain things a certain way, and many times those things don't turn out the way we wish. One of the main reasons that they don't is because oftentimes our higher power is guiding us in one direction, and we ignore the guidance and try to do things our own way. We try it our own way over and over again, and things still don't turn out the way we wish. This happens because our higher power is still guiding us to do certain things the way they *should* be done. So, if you feel at times that you are repeating the same old things over again, remember to let go and let God.

Notes

_____

_____

_____

_____

_____

_____

_____

_____

_____

_____

_____

_____

SESSION 24

PEACE OF MIND AND PEACEFUL HEART

PEACE OF MIND AND A peaceful heart do exist. Peace of mind is something that comes with being at peace with yourself, your life, and the things and individuals that you are involved with. Having a peaceful heart consists of being at peace with yourself and at peace with your life. Have inner peace and also extend peace to other people that you meet. For the most part, as you extend peace to others, peace often finds its way back to you. Learn to give yourself peace and learn to extend peace to others because there may be someone else in need of the peaceful blessings that you will have to offer.

Spending time with my grandchildren brings peace to me and allows me to feel totally relaxed. Knowing the peacefulness that I extend to them helps ensure that they will do the same with other people. How do I know this? I constantly witness them displaying their peaceful energy and mannerisms at an early age.

Have peace of mind and a peaceful heart; then let your peace be a blessing to someone else.

NOTES

_____

_____

_____

_____

_____

_____

_____

_____

_____

_____

_____

_____

_____

SESSION 25

PASS IT ON

NOW THAT YOU'VE REACHED THE end of *He Can't Make You Happy*, you realize that you are your happiness and that you are the only one responsible for your happiness. Just like in the *Wizard of Oz*, you've had it in you all along. Now it's time to pass it on. We are on this planet to help others and to make it a better place to live. Now it's your turn to help others who may have the challenges that you once had. However, before you begin to assist someone else, be sure that you've read this book at least three times because you may pick up on some points that you missed in your first or second reading.

I want to wholeheartedly congratulate you in giving yourself the gift of learning that has been laid out for you. I purposely did not include the word *chapter* in the table of contents, because these are not chapters; they are classes. Just as you would sit in a class or take an online course, you've just experienced an in-hand class. I know that you will be fine, even if it takes a little more time than expected. By the way, I'm still working on me, and so are many others.

So, until we meet again, may you be filled with total joy and happiness.

No More

NO MORE UNHAPPINESS

NO MORE SETTLING FOR LESS

NO MORE NEGATIVE THINKING

NO MORE NONBELIEVING

NO MORE EXCUSES

NO MORE SELF-LIES

NO MORE SELF-DOUBT

NO MORE SELF-PITY

NO MORE BAD ISSUES

NO MORE DRAMA

NO MORE BS

NO MORE BLAMING

SELF-ASSESSMENT

_____

_____

_____

_____

_____

_____

_____

_____

_____

_____

_____

_____

_____

_____

_____

_____

_____

_____

_____

_____

_____

_____

_____

_____

_____

_____

_____

_____

_____

_____

_____

_____

ABOUT THE AUTHOR

Skip Bailey, the author of *You Are Outstanding and Unstoppable*, is a professional certified life coach, relationship coach, and a certified drug and alcohol recovery coach. He is a local radio talk show host in New Jersey and a former local talk show host in Princeton, New Jersey. Skip, a professional bass guitarist and event producer, along with being a network marketing professional, is originally from Cape Charles, Virginia, and currently lives in New Jersey. He coaches clients in multiple cities and states along with hosting seminars and workshops.

Contact Skip Bailey as your Personal Life Coach

And

Relationship Coach

1skipbailey@gmail.com

www.skipbailey.com

www.twitter.com/1skipbailey

Facebook: Skip Bailey Official

Instagram: 1skipbailey

Linkedin.com

SKYPE: 1skipbailey

For your Health & Wellness needs

And

Career Opportunity

Visit:

www.totallifechanges.com/7health

www.iasotea.com/7health

Lose 5 Pounds In 5 Days

Why Can't He See . . .

Angela L. Neely

Why can't he see . . . the hurt woman in me. I'm trying my best to be all he needs me to be. I have so much love to give it's true . . . but why am I'm constantly giving and getting nothing in return from you.

My love is so deep, I give all my heart and soul . . . why can't he see this relationship is taking a toll . . . on my very being. But he simply can't see . . . there's something so deep within me.

My heart aches for his love, but he'd rather stretch himself so thin, and I'm the one that gets hurt in the end. You have something everyone else wants he says (his time) but why should I have to share with so many others? That's the real crime!

He says "I'm a man, it's what we do," but somehow this man just doesn't have a clue . . . If the shoe's on the other foot, you're in so much pain. But are you the only one with a heart? Or am I simply a game?

There are so many other men I can turn to, but why can't you understand . . . I want and love you! But he won't open his eyes . . . so here is my dilemma . . . I love a man that can't see. He loves me, but he's hurting me.

I'd give the world if he asks me to, my heart breaks daily because you'll never find a woman that loves you more than I do.

I'm hurt, He's killing me . . . through it all, like Maya Angelou, Still I rise, but you could never tell because of the tears in my eyes. I'm slowly falling down . . . My friends say he's changing me and my voice has no sound.

I'm like a broken record . . . because he refuses to hear, why am I wasting my time . . . what's the real fear?

You never miss a good thing until it's gone, but is that my real fear . . . I don't want to be alone. So, I settle for his behavior and think to myself it's ok . . . but I feel so damn bad at the end of the day.

Crying myself to sleep, tossing and turning in my bed, doing everything possible to get this man out of my head. Torturing myself for what I continue to say, but somehow I'm still here like a lost and lonely stray.

People say its low self-esteem, (NAH) . . . I'm a LEO, it's my world! I just want this man to love me, like I'm his favorite girl. Make me feel special treat me, like I treat you! **Come on fellas . . . Is that so hard to do?**

His love takes me places I've never ever been . . . the way he makes me feel my whole world transcends. I can hear you saying (like Usher) she's got it bad, but make no mistakes . . . I'm the best this brother ever had!

I require much more than just his touch. Feel my heart and know that it's been broken too much. I treat him better than he's ever been treated before, but I think it's time to close this chapter and walk on out this door.

Why can't he see that I'd do whatever he required of me . . . I've given my heart, my soul . . . I'd love him for all eternity. I want to shout out to the world about my love . . . but instead . . . I'm in a cage like a dove.

Simply because so many others can say the same, and he has the audacity to worry about who's calling my name??!! Why can't he see the pain he's causing me . . . or maybe it's time I open my own brown eyes and see . . .

This relationship is really one sided and the pain is much more than I can bear. I'm beginning not to feel a thing and worse off, not even care. I've given so much of me, it seems like a total waste . . . and I don't want to do anything in haste . . . So I took my time to think . . .

And . . . FINALLY . . . I got the strength to walk away! It hasn't been easy and requires me daily on my knees to pray.

So, I'll be strong enough not to answer his late night calls . . . (let's keep it real) you know the deal; that'll make me fall . . . back into the same thing over and over again . . . No . . . I'm not going to answer . . . this time I'm going to win!

Love is a mother . . . (let me shut my mouth) . . . but we're all adults . . . Y'all know what I'm talking about!! He killed me softly, I can't even stand here and lie, that's why you see the tears still forming in my eyes.

And what doesn't kill you makes you stronger (so they say). But the good thing is I'm still capable of loving the "right man" one day.

People said girl you're crazy, I would've been left that fool, but it's always easier said than done when you're not walking in

109

my shoes. So take what people say literally with a grain of salt, just because you fall in love . . . doesn't mean you're at fault.

It means your heart is pure and your love is true; it doesn't depict the BEAUTIFUL Person inside of you. Forgive and move on, is the best advice I have to GIVE . . . Trust me . . . (It's HIS loss) . . . You go ahead and LIVE!!

AND YEAH . . . I still miss him from time to time . . . but my heart is strengthened and I have total piece of mind. The love we shared was so real, and in time . . . broken hearts can heal.

I did what was needed to protect mine and live in peace . . . I gave him more than he was willing to give me . . . He didn't need to open his eyes . . . **Sisters . . . I was the one that needed to see!!**

So, I finally put on my glasses, opened my eyes . . . and I was gone!! Now he's calling, crying, telling me that I was wrong . . . (But y'all know the words to that old Badu song) . . . I think You better call . . . TYRONE!!!

You Get What You Tolerate

Angela L. Neely

For so many years I tolerated the lies, fake alibi's and many a night I stayed up and cried . . . Now I'm sitting here pen in hand asking myself WHY?

What happened to me that I longer felt like a Queen, and to be subjected to a man that was downright disrespectful and mean.

I simply tolerated too much of his mess, and now it seems as if I've totally regressed . . . Into a woman I don't seem to know . . . oh but can you really hear me though?

I'm trying to figure out in my mind what I did wrong, and what would make me tolerate his nonsense for so long.

So allow me to go back in time and begin to readjust my mind. When we met, it was like a dream come true. Funny how "LOVE" will play tricks on you.

All the time I thought it was just me. No one said anything about 3.

He claimed they're **"Friends"** and you have them, too. Yeah, but my friends have boundaries, Dude.

He says **I'm unapologetically me.** That should have been the time for me to run and set myself free.

But, no, this HEART kept on beating until one night, he and I got into a serious fight. He came from this so-called "FRIEND" with his clothes inside/out and claimed: "I'm a man; you know what it's about."

Even after that I continued to tolerate him and it got much worse, to the point where I lost myself as if under a curse.

I realized you get what you tolerate and I had simply had enough. Told him to leave and pack all of his stuff.

I could no longer stand to see his face, and at this point I felt like I was the disgrace.

How could I be so stupid and let him walk all over me? It was something I merely TOLERATED you see . . .

Love is a many-splendored thing. But was it really "love" with the disrespect he would bring?

I kept putting up with his lies and all of his excuses, until I realized he'll never change . . . and I was like two fingers in the air—"DUECES!"

Gone like the wind and I never looked back. You'll realize when you're free . . . it wasn't worth all the flack.

But why did I allow him to treat me that way? It started from the very beginning . . . **I TOLERATED IT** . . . is all I can say!

When you get tired and simply can't take it anymore, you'll understand it wasn't really a LOVE worth fighting for.

A man will only treat you the way you allow him to, so start off with STANDARDS and make sure that he's true . . . or you know what you must do.

I tolerated him for way too long, and now that I'm free no time for his sad songs. The only thing I have to say is . . . LEAVE ME ALONE!

I could say wasted years and wasted tears, but experience is what it was . . . and trust I'm not tolerating anything going forward but that 1st Corinthians Love.

I'm so very grateful that the LOVE within me didn't turn to HATE, but one final warning: **You Get What You Tolerate!**

He Can't Make You Happy

Angela L. Neely

He can't make you happy—nor is he supposed to—but somehow when in "LOVE" we pass the responsibility of our HAPPINESS, this I found to be true.

I always dreamed of the "perfect love" as a little girl, figuring I'd meet the man who would make me the happiest woman in the world.

After more than a few heartbreaks, becoming depressed and blue, I came to realize that happiness comes not from the other person, but happiness comes from YOU!

We (as women) have the tendency to place the blame without first looking within, which is usually where it all begins.

You see, like so many others, I too had to learn the hard way, which enables me to write about my experiences today.

I always placed my ability to be "HAPPY" on someone else, when all along I wasn't really happy with myself.

Whether it's our hair, skin, or our weight, it's always something about ourselves that we hate.

So instead of worrying about a man, I began working on me—that was the ultimate plan.

The things I hated about myself I began to change, and my priorities, I had to rearrange.

First, I cut all the perm out of my hair. It was so liberating and free . . . I didn't have a care, for once it was all about me! Funny thing, that's how it's supposed to be.

Everyone thought something was wrong; my brothers were constantly blowing up my phone . . .

I laughed so hard because it was only hair, but if you could've seen people and their stares!

It was all part of the transformation into the new and improved me. There was only one goal: making and keeping myself . . . Happy!

As we all know, so many people are afraid of what others have to say; it's one of the primary reasons so many are in "bondage" today.

I kept on moving forward—didn't allow what people thought to stop me in my tracks. I'm very satisfied that I never once looked back.

I changed in so many ways and began to accomplish some things I always loved to do: traveling, writing, and pretty much anything I chose to.

As women, we often take care of everyone else, so often neglecting ourselves. It's okay to put yourself first; make that your number 1 priority and be steadfast in your journey.

Now that I think about it . . . I can't fathom how I put my HAPPINESS in his hands, when clearly being HAPPY has nothing to do with a man!

Like Dorothy from the *Wizard of Oz*, everything she wanted and desired was on the inside; once I came to the realization, tears of joy. . . I did cry.

Once you truly love yourself . . . you'll clearly understand. You won't ever place your HAPPINESS in any person, and especially not a man.

Today, I'm thoroughly HAPPY and you ask the question why? It's no longer about him opening his eyes to see or my tolerating anything. It's all about what makes my heart sing!

And that song is simply: **The Greatest Love of All . . . Was Inside of Me!"**

OF COURSE HE CAN'T MAKE YOU HAPPY; IT'S ALL ABOUT SELF-DISCOVERY . . .

Contact Angela Neely: Email angeladar1@aol.com
Facebook: Angela L. Neely